Profound Impact

Forging Success Beyond Circumstance

Conrad Wilson with Julie Pershing

Gallivant Press

Dedication

I would like to thank Jesus Christ, my Lord and personal Savior for allowing me to live and continually blessing me. Because of His grace, I can share my story to give hope and help to someone who is hurting on this side of life. My favorite verse is Jeremiah 29:11: *For I know the plans I have for you, declares the LORD, plans to prosper you and not to harm you, plans to give you hope and a future.* I understand where much is given, much is required.

I dedicate this book to my loving children Bryson and McKenzi, and my two beautiful granddaughters Harper and Halle. I love all of you to the moon and back. Without you my life would not be complete. Love you, Dad/Pop and Grandpa Wilson.

A personal dedication on this project goes to my Momma, Mattie K. Wilson. She instilled the core values of leadership and responsibility in my life and taught me the importance of getting up when life knocks you down. RIP 1998. We did it, Momma! I love you always, "Mr. Clean".

Two of the most important role models in my life are Gerald S. Rawlins and his lovely wife Doreen. I believe God sent them to guide me and to help me understand twig bending. They helped to shape me into the man I am today.

A special thank you to my 93-year-old guardian angel, my good friend and confidant, Jack B. Kisinger. Jack gave me valuable advice, which allowed me to move forward and forgive my birth father. He helped me to realize God is my Father, and what He has ordained, no human being has the power to stop. Jack said to me, "Conrad, you are destined to change the world one person at a time". And I believe and receive it in Jesus name, Amen!

I would like to thank the many friends, family, coaches, and a host of guardian angels who poured water on the seeds planted in me as I journeyed through life to become the man I am today. I want to extend a personal and sincere thanks to you for seeing something in me I couldn't see myself.

Finally, I want to thank Julie Pershing and Gallivant press for your hard work and dedication to this Project. I couldn't have done it without you. You're the Best!

I believe this project is about Grace not race. We must become the conduit to connect people to a cause larger than themselves. Remember TEAM - Together Everyone Achieves More!

Conrad Wilson

Forward

The first time I saw Conrad (Larry) Wilson, he was playing in a basketball tournament. I learned he was fifteen years old and was schooling young men two and three years older. Larry was the best player on the floor, but he did not appear to be having a good time. He scowled at the referee, glared at the other team, barely spoke to his teammates, and he shot a lot more than he passed.

"What's up with this kid?" I wondered. "Big talent, possible trouble."

Several years later I learned what was up with Larry Wilson. He played two years at the local community college where my brother coached, and then he was recruited to play for Corban University where I've taught since 1973.

Larry married a young beauty named Robin, and they had a baby boy named Bryson. The high school hothead had become an engaging young man with a smile as quick as his jump shot.

Conrad was still a dynamic player, and I enjoyed getting to know him. In conversations between classes or in my office, I pieced together his life story and came to understand why he'd been so angry, so quick to bristle.

From the beginning, he'd faced tough challenges. He was a black kid in a very white town in a mostly white state, one with a racial history fraught with difficulty and danger for him. His birth mother disappeared from his life when he was a small boy. His father lost a hand to a gunshot blast. One night someone fired gunshots into the bedroom where little Larry was sleeping. Small wonder his default setting for dealing with the world was through confrontation.

He has grown beyond his old ways of handling things. His maturing faith and experience have brought about a very different person. He still has the old energy—it seems like the guy never stops moving—but a new sense of self and a new sense of purpose. The fiery hooper goes by Conrad now. He is a shooting coach, something of an entrepreneur, and now an author, telling his story as an assurance to others our difficulties need neither limit us nor define us.

It's as though he can still shoot but he is also happy to pass the ball. He has a complete game now—and a lot more fun.

Jim Hills
Professor of Humanities, Corban University

Dr. Hills has been bringing the written word alive for Corban University students for over 40 years. Before becoming a faculty member in 1973, Dr. Hills taught at his alma mater, The Master's College. He has published sixty articles, and two books, *Garage Sale of the Mind and Other Opinions* (2015) and *The Car(di)nal Mind* (2015).

Our Struggles in life
are simply a tool
in creating
who we are.

Focus on the game.

- Conrad Wilson

Table of Contents

My past has
prepared me
for my present
life.

No matter what,
I am blessed.

- Conrad Wilson

CHAPTER ONE

Truth

Growing up with an alcoholic father who often was physically and verbally abusive, I've struggled with depression and the associated symptoms throughout my life.

The consequences of childhood episodes of abuse and ongoing patterns of stress followed me into adulthood. I didn't have the skills or knowledge to know how to deal with them or how to transition successfully into a well-adjusted adult.

I married my childhood sweetheart in 1987. Over the next few years, my stress level increased. I was working in a high-pressure job, and now I had a family to support. I didn't know how to work through my issues without getting angry or upset with my wife and children. I didn't have a role model growing up to teach me how to be a good father and provider. I mistakenly thought I had a reasonable handle on things since I wasn't being violent or abusing alcohol.

I had a hard time maintaining a sense of normalcy and found myself lying around in my own misery and pain.

Finally, I admitted I couldn't do it alone and set up an appointment with my doctor. He prescribed several types of medications to help me with the chemical imbalance with which I had been struggling. I became less overwhelmed and learned to manage my stress level day by day.

I started my medication regime and felt better. I developed a false sense of security and began drinking. Before long, I started self-medicating with alcohol. I told myself it made me comfortable at social gatherings. Before long, I drank more and more trying to refresh the comfortable feelings I experienced the first few times.

I continued drinking and soon I quit taking my prescribed medications. I was spiraling out of control and drank alcohol to help me cope. I have known other people who acted free from stress and worry when they drank, and I figured it should work for me, too. It didn't take long before my marriage suffered. My wife and I argued over little issues and the arguments and problems escalated. Before long our family, friends, and even our children noticed.

I wanted to be the husband and father my family needed me to be. I attended church and social events. I cut back on the alcohol. I continued to drink, but nothing to the extent of what I had been doing. I saw my physician regularly. He put me on a new medication plan to help with the depression and stress. The medications made me anxious and uneasy. I avoided counseling; it embarrassed me. I wanted no one to be aware I struggled with my marriage and in other areas of my life. It seemed as if everything was falling apart.

By 1998, my downward spiral intensified. I stopped listening to my doctor and started self-medicating with alcohol and marijuana. I had recently worked through my step-mother Mattie's death and the alienation from some of my siblings after her death.

October 16, 2004 is the day the darkness overwhelmed me. My wife Robin had just left the house to drop our daughter McKenzi off at school for a volleyball road trip. She planned to stop by her sister's house and spend time before coming back home. My son Bryson and his girlfriend Sara were visiting from California and had gone out for breakfast.

I was home alone. The pain and the heartache were overwhelming. I didn't think about how my loved ones would feel after my death. I wanted the pain to stop, and I attempted suicide with a firearm. My father gave me a 12-gauge shotgun just weeks before the shooting. I walked into the master bedroom closet and started fooling around with the gun. The gun fired, and the blast hit me in the neck and face. I woke from the explosion and looked in the mirror. When I saw my reflection, I became delusional and disoriented. I reloaded the gun and found my way into the garage.

I remember thinking "I can't go on like this" before I put the gun to the left side of my chest, closed my eyes and pulled the trigger. My son was 20, and my daughter just 16 when I tried to end my life.

I called my wife and told her I had been shot and needed help. My son's friend Jason Summers called and somehow, I answered the phone. He said I was incoherent, but he understood I was asking for help before the call disconnected. He called me back several times and when I didn't answer he rushed to our home. Bryson and Sara returned from breakfast at about the same time.

I remember the garage door opening and seeing the paramedics rushing toward me. I saw Robin getting out of the car. Everything moved in slow motion. I had an out-of-body experience and found myself standing in the yard watching the paramedics trying to save my life. It was so surreal. The ambulance rushed me to Salem Hospital where they have a Level II trauma center. I suffered two point-blank, self-inflicted 12-gauge shotgun wounds, one to the left side of my chest and one to the right side of my head. They life-flighted me to Oregon Health Science University (OSHU) in Portland. They told my family to prepare for the worst. I was in a medically induced coma, on life support and not expected to recover or regain a normal life.

I woke up after 33 days in a coma, with revitalized hope and a strong desire to recover. Ten days later, I was released from the hospital. I and went back to work just 62 days after the shooting.

After leaving the hospital, I went home to recover before starting counseling and found I was even more depressed. How could I be depressed? I survived being shot at point-blank range and I'm living on the 9th hole of a golf course in a beautiful gated subdivision.

One day after taking a shower, I looked at myself and couldn't believe I was struggling again, even while taking medication. Not knowing at the time, the medication had caused or provoked the behavior to want just to check out.

I loved my kids and I loved my wife; we had a great life and things were going well. My wife Robin was managing a bank, my son was a superstar football player, and my daughter was a high school student.

I went into the closet in the master suite and tied a dress shirt tie around my neck and tried my best to hang myself. And I just couldn't. I remember getting numb, tingling in my head. But there was a small voice and it kept saying you've got more, you need to do more, you can be more. I don't know if it was the Holy Spirit or my subconscious, I didn't know what it was, but it was almost audible.

I took the noose from around my neck and I sat there and cried. I looked in the mirror and I said, God, if you can help me through this, I will walk it out and I will do whatever it takes. I will face the unfaceable, I'll stand in front of people and give You the glory and honor for what's happened. Within a couple of weeks, I was in counseling and they started slowly taking me off the medications which were causing my delusional thoughts about death.

And it was at this point, I got up. Like the song says we fall down, but we get up. And I got up. I started by mowing my yard. I could mow the front yard, and soon I could mow the backyard. I started walking, I could walk halfway around the block, then I could walk the whole half mile entrance into the subdivision. I began walking the loop; it was a mile long. I went back to the gym.

I was taking progressive steps. Reading positive and uplifting books and articles, and associating myself with people who had a larger outlook on life. I returned to athletics because I knew the skills were counter transferable. Meaning I could redirect the knowledge and skills I learned as an athlete to work for me in my personal life. If I was a great basketball player and people were playing a zone defense against me or boxing me in, one guy would be guarding and the other part of the team would play a zone. I overcame all of it by using those same skills. I remember going to the free throw line in my mind and having 10 seconds to shoot the ball. I started taking timeouts and thinking and stretching.

And soon I was limbering up and I started to gain weight. I believed people were seeing results. They could not believe I had been shot. They did not understand why I wanted to die.

I returned to my job as a Juvenile Parole & Probation Officer, just after the new year in 2005. Returning to work in the corrections field is very difficult after a suicide attempt. I was under intense scrutiny. My coworkers and community partners didn't know how to talk to me about what had happened.

People didn't know what happened, no one was there at the time I was shot, and they all drew on speculation. There was no suicide note. One day it just happened. I say to you and anyone who may listen, we don't know why we want to quit, we just want the pain to be over.

Emotionally, I was damaged and I was continuing to recover from the gunshot wounds. With a hole in my chest and losing about 100 pounds, I was working and presenting in the courtroom.

Attending intense trauma counseling helped me understand what happened and gave me the skills I needed to cope and move forward with my life.

I kept my composure, took my prescribed medications, and attended counseling twice a week to learn how to deal with the mounting stress and strain. I was under constant observation, but I had a strong desire to succeed. I had a family to support and a mortgage to pay. I wanted to be well and move past this horrible incident.

I never wanted to die. I never wanted to leave my children behind. I wanted to raise my son to become the man he was supposed to be. I'm grateful, I got a second chance to be an example to him and many other people. I give encouragement, I'm here before you today and I'm honored. It's a miracle. Now the same success carried over into my life. I've had peaks and valleys, but I have more peaks now and I'm climbing. It's been a progressive upswing in my life. I live by the rule "I do as I say". And I also "Do as I do". People have convinced me and I'm trying to get the message out to the public, somebody needs to be encouraged by the journey through change I went through.

What the caterpillar calls the end, the butterfly calls the beginning. And it's what happened to me, my old self died. I flew away and I haven't looked back. I'm mindful of the reference point which got me where I'm at today and propels me to keep going. We live in a confused world where people struggle with so many things. I know of everyday people, and famous actors and actresses who have taken their own lives, or their spouses have killed themselves. But I believe just like me, they didn't want to die. They didn't want to leave their loved ones behind. What they wanted was an opportunity to get the pain to stop.

My mission is to provide a plan so you can move forward no matter what goes on around you. We have an opportunity to get out of our rut. I'm careful now, I choose my ruts wisely because you could be in the rut for the rest of your life. I look at my life from the positive and live moment by moment.

It's a very emotional for me to talk about my journey. I'm compassionate and I feel I have a responsibility to share my story with anyone who needs hope and change in their life. If we can dissect the elements needed to overcome adversity, we can help others to reach in and find what they need to heal from the pain.

I'm going to simply say it like this "I'm an AmeriCAN not an AmeriCAN'T". I can succeed. I can overcome. I believe in people as people have believed in me. I seek out people who have evidence in their life of overcoming hardship. The best sign of a leader is one who can get up after an adverse situation, and I'm not boastful about it - I'm thankful for it.

Lifelong effects of abuse and neglect can create a perfect storm of stress and overwhelm. I now recognize how the severity of my despair impacted my children and my wife.

To fully comprehend how I came to the point of wanting to end my life, I needed to look at the physical and mental damage I was subjected to throughout my childhood and into adulthood. More than anything, I wanted to learn how to build a life beyond my circumstances.

If you're thinking about suicide, are worried about a friend or loved one, or would like emotional support, the Lifeline network is available 24/7 across the United States.

I've looked for you
in everyone I've
ever met.

I imagined
you were
looking for me, too.

- Julie Pershing

CHAPTER TWO

Shirley Sonya Boland

My birth mother Shirley Sonya Boland was of French Creole and Puerto Rican descent. She was soft spoken and beautiful.

Her grandfather, Dr. Robert Boland was the first African-American doctor in Virginia in the late 1800s.

Her father, Jesse Lee Boland married Vernice Hearty. They had two sons and four daughters. Jesse Lee Boland became a skilled pilot and made his living as a fortune teller with a stage name of 'Master X'.

Vernice and Jesse later divorced, and my grandmother moved to California with the girls and made a life there. Jesse stayed in Virginia with the two boys, Jesse Lee and Michael 'Conrad' Boland. My mother's brother Conrad was her favorite and she named me Conrad in his honor.

Shirley Sonya Boland

Shirley was a single mother, a minority woman raising a baby in Los Angeles in the 1960s. I was her only child and she loved me. She did not have much contact with my father. One day when I was 18 months old, my father stopped by unexpectedly and picked me up to go have ice cream. He didn't bring me back home. He abducted me and changed my name to Larry. My mother's life would never be the same after that terrible day.

As the days turned to months, and the months into years, she thought she would never see me again. I don't know how she made it through those dark days. It's hard for me as a father to comprehend the heartache and pain of losing your only child.

Conrad Wilson

When I was 23 years old, my godparents helped me hire a private investigator to find my birth mother. Incredibly, he found her still living in Los Angeles. When my mother heard a man by the name of Larry Wilson had been trying to locate her, it terrified her.

She didn't know he had changed my name to Larry after he kidnapped me, and no one had called me Conrad for many years. My mother was afraid of my father for most of her adult life; she told me she was sure one day Larry Wilson would find her and hurt her.

The private investigator helped me to establish contact with my grandmother, Vernice. We talked for two weeks before she was certain it wasn't a hoax, and I really was Conrad. She decided we should set up a meeting between me and my birth mother.

Vernice Boland, maternal grandmother

I flew to Los Angeles as soon as we finalized the plans to meet. I stayed at the Bonaventure Hotel; my mother came to the hotel to meet me. I waited outside for her, and I still can clearly remember the moment - I recognized my mom the instant she drove up. She rolled the window down, and said, "Hello Conrad." So easy and casual as if over 20 years hadn't passed since we'd last seen each other. I could see in her eyes, the pain and suffering, and most of all, her love. We hugged, we laughed, we cried. When I got into the car, she reached over and with her voice shaking, she repeated over and over, "I'm just so nervous, you're so beautiful, you're so handsome."

Conrad and Shirley, the day they reunited

It was very emotional for me to find my birth mother after all those years. I spent the week getting reacquainted with her. She told me stories about my childhood and our family. She shared pictures of me as a baby and a small child. Looking at the pictures, I could only think of how she saved those old worn photos of me and I felt her pain.

I finally learned my true family history during my week in Los Angeles. My parents never married; she was a single mother from the moment of my birth. They met in Los Angeles when my father tried to pursue a career opportunity with the Harlem Globe Trotters. She worked as a hostess at the Chapman Grill, and they met when he came in for lunch one day.

Sonya and Larry were in a relationship for less than six months. She told me it didn't take long for her to figure out he was a liar and a player, and she wanted no association with him. When his gig with the Globe Trotters didn't work out, he left California and moved on to his next pursuit.

I learned Larry frequently contacted my mom after he kidnapped me. He had the nerve to manipulate her into sending him money by telling her I was in the hospital and he needed help with expenses. She didn't have much, but she sent him what little money she could. Not only did he take her child from her, he lied and told her I was critically ill. She had no way of knowing the truth. Another heartbreak.

My mom married my stepfather Bob Lynch, 5 years after Larry abducted me. She and Bob had no children. She worked as a food service manager for the Los Angeles Unified School District until she retired.

Shirley and Bob Lynch

After I reunited with my biological mother, she asked to contact my stepmother. When they talked on the phone, my mother thanked Mattie for keeping me safe and for loving me. These women rose above an impossible situation to show their love for me and found a shared appreciation and love for each other. I witnessed grace and forgiveness when they talked that day.

In 2003, I received a call from the Los Angeles County Coroner. My heart sank, my children were in Los Angeles at the time and immediately I thought something terrible had happened. Only the call wasn't about my kids, it was my mother. The Coroner called to tell me she had passed away.

My stepfather called right after I finished talking with the coroner. Her death devastated him, and he had been drinking heavily. Through his sobbing, he told me "They need to take my gun, please tell them to take the gun. I want to be with your mom."

I was in Oregon when I received the call. I packed a few things as quickly as I could and drove straight through to Los Angeles. My first stop was at the townhouse where my mother and Bob had lived for 30 years. I needed to know what happened; I wanted to see her. Bob told me "No, you don't want to go there, she wanted you to remember her the way she was."

Before she passed, my mother received in-home nursing care. The nurses hired to care for her took advantage of this dying woman and her grieving husband. When I arrived, there were few of her possessions left, they stole her prized possessions and had even taken her jewelry. The one thing left for me to remember her by was a musical jewelry box in the shape of a piano. I took the music box and locked it in my car; I didn't want to lose my only memento which belonged to her.

The coroner transported my mother's body to Armstrong Funeral Home. I called the funeral home to set up a time to pay my respects, but they wouldn't tell me anything because they listed my stepfather as her next of kin. By law, the next of kin is the only one who can give permission for someone to view the body. My stepfather was drowning his grief in alcohol and in no condition to grant permission. I went to the funeral home, anyway. The funeral director stepped out of his office to talk with me. He was sympathetic and offered to contact the Los Angeles County Coroner to confirm our relationship.

The heat was sweltering in Los Angeles when she died. The day I stopped at the funeral home the temperature hovered over 100 degrees. My mother passed away a few days before they granted approval for me to view her. The funeral home told me her body was being prepared for cremation. I imagined she would be in a tranquil, refrigerated room. I visualized a serene setting, with soft background music playing.

A woman who worked at the funeral home entered the reception area to guide me to her. We walked through a long maze of hallways and wound our way into a garage. The garage was suffocatingly hot; I was sweating from the heat and from nervousness. The air was humid and heavy, and I felt every breath. My heart was beating in my ears. There was no cool room, it was not serene. I recall thinking it wasn't a proper place for my mother to be in her final time here on earth.

We finally reached a ramp and stopped in the stifling hot garage. The woman said, "Here's your mother, I'm warning you - it's been two days." She said it nonchalantly as if I should understand what she meant. As I stood at the base of a concrete ramp, I didn't know what to expect, I took a deep breath. I looked up at the gurney at the top of the ramp, and I could see a body on the table. I approached the ramp, and halfway up I saw her. I didn't recognize her. I stared in horror at her swollen head and the water running out of her eyes. My mother's entire body was weeping. I turned and struggled to run. It seemed as if everything was happening in slow motion. I could hear the woman from the funeral home laughing as I blindly scrambled to find my way out of there. She grabbed my arm, saying "It's all right, it's all right, baby. Are you all right?"

Somehow, I found my way back to the car. When I unlocked the door, my mother's music box was playing. I believe her spirit was telling me she was there, and everything would be fine. At this moment, I resolved to use my given name of Conrad to honor her memory.

Three years later, my stepfather, Bob passed away. Once again, I received a call from the Los Angeles County Coroner. They asked me where to take his body. Not knowing where else to go, I told them Armstrong Funeral Home. They transported my mother to the same place after she died.

Before Bob died, his friends tried to convince him to put the remaining estate in my name. He had no children, and I was his closest relative. We talked about it, but he never followed through with making any changes. I returned to Los Angeles after he passed to help take care of his affairs. Bob had money in the bank, along with stocks and bonds held by his attorney for safekeeping.

Bob Lynch and Conrad Wilson

When I contacted Bob's attorney, he wasn't aware of any other immediate family. I completed the paperwork required to disburse the estate, and we went to probate court. The week the estate should have settled, Bob's great-niece came forward and challenged the will. Bob's estate ended up being split between the great-niece and her children. They distributed the money among the heirs and there was nothing left.

Over the course of working on the estate, Bob's attorney and I become well acquainted. We stayed in touch and became friends. He told me someday this experience would be a blessing, and I would receive so much more than money. I didn't know it then, but he was right.

Circumstance
does not
make me,
it reveals me.

- William James

CHAPTER THREE

LD Wilson

L. D. Wilson is my biological father. He grew up in the small town of Kilgore, Texas. When he was born, he didn't have a proper name, only the initials L.D. At some point, while growing up he chose the name Larry Darnell Wilson and goes by Larry.

My grandfather's name was John Wilson, he passed when I was young. I didn't get to meet him; I've never even seen a picture of him. My grandmother's name was Lottie Wilson Daniels. She remarried after her husband John died. My father's only brother, Jimmy Daniels is 20 years younger. Jimmy is a decent, hardworking man. He works in the oil fields and still lives in Kilgore, Texas.

I met my Grandmother Lottie my sophomore year in high school. My father had been sending her pictures of me over the years, I didn't realize it until I walked into her house. She had newspaper clippings and pictures of me playing basketball; a shrine all over her living room walls. It felt a little unnerving since I had never met her, but she seemed to know a lot about me. I only saw her one other time before her death in 2005.

Larry attended to Fredonia High School in Kilgore, Texas. He played basketball and was popular in school. His girlfriend was a cheerleader. In his senior year of high school, his girlfriend got pregnant. His first-born child was a daughter named Brenda Moss. Larry did not stick around to be a father or to support or help raise his daughter.

Larry was a talented basketball player, and he traveled to Los Angeles and try out for the Harlem Globetrotters. He met my mother Shirley while he was in California trying out for the team. When he didn't make the cut with the Globetrotters, he returned to Texas. My mother didn't tell him she was pregnant with me before he left California.

Larry wanted to get out of Texas and joining the Air Force would be his way out. A commissioned officer and a member of the Air Force basketball team, they stationed him at Luke Air Force Base in Glendale, Arizona.

One month after I was born, Larry came to Los Angeles to meet his first-born son. Larry and my mother spent the weekend in a hotel, I was so small my mother used blankets to make a bed for me in the dresser drawer, and it's where I slept.

Larry didn't come around again until I was 18 months old. He showed up unexpectedly at our house and said he wanted to take me for ice cream. My mother said it surprised her to see him there, but it made her happy he wanted to spend time with me. He was a stranger, but he was my father, so she let me go with him - the biggest regret of her life.

When Larry picked me up, he didn't want to spend time with me or take me out for ice cream. He kidnapped me and took me from a loving home and everything I had ever known. My mother told me he threatened to hurt her if she reported him to the police. He stole her only child.

After kidnapping me, my father promptly changed my name to Larry. He knew my mother would not have been looking for a child named Larry Wilson. He was a mean man, calculating and cruel.

Larry took me from Los Angeles to Arizona where he had a girlfriend named Mattie. Larry met Mattie and her children while stationed at Luke Air Force Base. When we arrived in Glendale, he thrust me into a blended family; my father, his girlfriend Mattie Katherine, and her 5 children.

I was too young to understand this start of a different life. I think about this little boy and wonder how many times he cried himself to sleep missing his mother. Many people could have helped me throughout my childhood, but no one did. Maybe they were scared, or they didn't know what to do. I'll never understand why no one stepped up to help this child.

I would ask, "when can I see my mom?" They would tell me it's just 'temporary' - for one year, 5 years, and then one day I realized - never. After a while, I quit asking. My whole childhood I struggled with not knowing.

I was a sophomore in high school before anyone talked to me about my birth mother. My father wouldn't tell me the truth, and no one else would either. They would say she's a pretty white woman. She's a pretty Mexican woman, a pretty Italian woman. The people who 'told' me about her had never even met her. So many lies.

My father remained distant throughout my childhood. He didn't build a relationship with me after kidnapping me. I believe he took me to hurt my mother. I was a possession to him. Even as I grew older, we never had a normal father-son relationship.

Larry was an alcoholic and an abuser. His unpredictable behavior and anger shaped my childhood. I remember many times when he abused me. He beat me with extension cords, a razor strap, and anything within reach including his hands and an occasional foot in the butt. When he walked through a door, you never knew if you should run and hide or just try to disappear into the room. It didn't take much to set him off, and no one could reason with him when he was angry.

I witnessed countless fights and the abuse he inflicted on Mattie. I can't count the times she shielded me from him during his drunken tirades, and he would beat her instead. The police came to our house almost every weekend responding to domestic disturbances. Larry became well known to the police, and people feared him because of his violent and dangerous behaviors.

I remember when I was five or six, he was in Independence Oregon. Migrant workers came to pick the crops and the older men and women would gather to drink and party at the end of the day. They would go to this gambling shack, like a Juke Joint. My father would roll dice. He gambled and played cards. He was flashy, and he had money. He is a good-looking man with a great smile and the women loved him.

We lived at 820 Cottage Street in Salem and I remember hearing all this commotion. It was the middle of the night and my brother and I were upstairs in bed. The foster kids were asleep in the basement. I heard screaming and crying and someone yelling "you've got to go to the hospital!"

I slipped downstairs and peeked into the bathroom. He was in the bathtub, and I remember seeing the tub was full of blood; the water was red, and it was full. He had been in a fight at the Shack and his left arm had been shot with a shotgun. I remember the scene - the chaos, the screaming, and crying.

He waited too long to go to the hospital, if he would have gone right away, they might have saved his arm. Later in life, he and the man who shot him became friends. They were gambling buddies. They were drunk, and my father lost his left arm.

I've seen pictures of my father with two arms, but I don't recall my father with two arms. I remember the first time he got a prosthetic arm. After he had the new arm, he got into an altercation with a guy. He shot at the guy and the guy shot back and blew up a propane tank. My father had lost his arm after being shot, and this time he thought he would die. He survived but didn't learn any lessons and nothing changed.

He became a Merchant Marine, working at the shipyards and bringing home $800 a week after taxes. It was a lot of money at the time. A country boy with all this money and a drinking problem.

I heard stories growing up how he had shot someone in Texas, but I was young and never knew the truth behind the stories. The rumor was it's why he wanted to leave Texas.

Someone had shot my father and he lost his arm, and it never humbled him. He always felt he had to be twice as tough. He carried a knife; he was known for carrying a switchblade or banana knife. I've seen him cut people. To this day he still carries a knife.

My father was sentenced to seven years in prison when I was a kid. They convicted him of firing a gun in public. He shot a guy on Cordon Road in Salem Oregon at a traffic light. It was road rage, but they didn't call it road rage back then. He plea-bargained, he could have ended up with a 15-year sentence and the court agreed to seven years. He didn't serve the whole seven years. He was trusted and a likable guy. He did three and a half years, and two years of the sentence was at a work release center in Forest Grove, Oregon. I remember going there and visiting him, he had his own barrack, like an army barrack.

He got in trouble later in life, he was caught possessing firearms. He was an ex-con in possession. My younger foster-brother took the rap for him one time. The cops came and raided the house, and he had all these guns. He went to jail. My younger brother said he was living there and took the rap of having these illegal guns. He's the same guy now he was back then, it's in his DNA. I don't think he'll ever change.

Ex-Convict Faces Weapons Charge

Larry D. Wilson, 37, 265 Lincoln St. SE, was arraigned Thursday in Marion County District Court on charges of being an ex-convict in possession of a firearm and carrying a concealed weapon.

Salem police said Wilson was arrested about 6:45 p.m. Wednesday after his car was stopped in the 500 block of Liberty Street NE. Police said a bag containing a .38 caliber pistol and a .22 caliber revolver were found in the car.

Oregon Statesman, Mar. 9, 1973

Without a doubt, losing his arm affected how he treated me. He was angry, and he wanted to prove himself. He felt like he was half a man. He had a chip on his shoulder, and I had the same chip. I felt like I had to prove myself to people. I channeled it into sports where he channeled it into "I'm a black man". The Civil Rights movement was happening at the time, and he was from Texas.

He thought after losing his arm he had to prove to everyone he was someone. It's never changed to this day he'll cuss you out, call you every name in the book and then come back and try to apologize. But the damage is done. He's an angry man.

He was a basketball player, in his younger years he tried out for the Harlem Globetrotters. I've always felt the loss of his arm later in life made him resent my basketball capabilities. At one of only four basketball high school basketball games he came to, it was senior night and he tried to pull me off the court. The girl I was dating at the time was Miss Oregon, her dad was a sheriff and he had to arrest my father at the game in front of everyone because he was disrupting the game.

I've always felt he was jealous of me because I was a good athlete. I learned to play basketball because I was channeling stress, depression, and abuse. So, I stayed on the court. He never told me I was a good athlete or a good basketball player.

To this day he tells other people he's proud of me but he's never told me. If he would have ever supported me or talked to me, I might have played 10 to 15 years in the NBA. But I had no support. No one at home told me how good I was, except for people outside my family who poured life and love into me. It was my Coaches and mentors who told me "you are somebody".

My father never made me believe I was good, and I felt he resented me. He'd say things to me like "you think you're the s.h.i.t." This is not how you nurture a child.

To this day we still don't have a relationship. Even as an adult, when I see him, he is still very disrespectful to me. I can't blame him, but ignorance doesn't require a response, and its ignorance. I will not play the game. I don't tell everybody, but the story is out, and it may help him know and others to know what I went through with him.

There was a time I wanted to kill him. I wanted to shoot him with his own gun, and I contemplated it. I'm serious because he beat the hell out of me and shaved my head when I had long hair. He decided it was my punishment, and then he said now you take your ass to school.

I waited for him. I thought about it, I knew where the gun and the bullets were. I was going to kill him. I would shoot him and say he abused me. In my heart, I wanted to kill him.

To this day, my brothers and sisters often ask, "Why did he treat you so differently? Why was he so mean to you?" I've been told they concluded he was jealous.

When he kidnapped me, he gave me the name Larry Wilson. I didn't know who I was, I knew I was something different. It's why I go by Conrad. I've had people ask if I'm related to Hook. They call him Hook because he has a hook arm. Are you related to Larry Wilson? I say he's my uncle, I wouldn't say he's my father. To this day, he introduces me to people and tells them I'm his oldest. They'll ask, who are you? And I'll ask him, who did you say I am? He knows I go by Conrad and he knows my mother named me Conrad. He was just a country bumpkin and doesn't know any different. I deal with it and I try to make the best of it.

The love and the nurturing of Mattie Wilson kept me from shooting him. I couldn't do it. I wanted to kill him, I was only 14 when I wanted to kill him. Only 14, and in junior high. I was practicing basketball at Willamette University because I was that good.

I was just a kid, and wanted to shoot him but I decided not to do it. It's a message for young kids, you can have feelings, but you don't have to act on them. You can be angry, and it's okay to be angry. But you need to learn how to channel the anger, and no one taught me. Mattie tried, but there was no one else teaching me. I think it's important to share my story to let other people realize even when you have those kinds of circumstances, you don't have to be bound by them

I've never told him I wanted to kill him; I've told others I wanted to kill him. I wanted the pain to stop. I've been a treatment manager at a youth correctional facility, I know parents who've gotten several years in prison for the things he did. Later in life when he had a second set of children, he got charged for whipping them. And it was when he finally stopped the abuse. Children's Services Division, now it's called CPS - Child Protective Services.

His other kids who are 10 years younger than me, were taken away from him because of his abuse.

Real Talk. He finally understood because the law said you will go to jail. There was a restraining order, all at the time I was in college living in Los Angeles. I've seen it all. But it made me better and thank God for Mattie, she always protected me. She would have conversations with me, she knew it hurt me.

He worked during the week and he would be mean as hell. Then when he got drunk, he'd be a happy drunk until he flipped the switch. He would invite all these people over and let his friends eat before we could eat. I remember it well, it's something I can never forget.

I made it I'm here for a reason. I'm supposed to encourage someone. I'm supposed to do all of the things and using my journey through change to help someone else. It's what Mattie always told me. She would say, "honey, you make sure you give back what was given to you". And she would say, "you don't owe me nothing". She would give me money or buy me things and tell me not to tell the other kids and don't tell your dad because he's a lunatic.

As a child and a young man, I was always looking for his approval. And even now as an adult. I hate to say it, but I want him to know I am somebody. More than he ever thought. I'd love to be President of the United States just to show him I made it. I swim upstream, not downstream.

Nothing will change if he approves of me, but part of me says show him anyway. Yes, it's an approval thing and for a kid, it's messed up. I don't feel like I became a man until I was about 30, as far as maturity and understanding. At the time my son was about 8 years old. It was a tough journey. I don't want to sound like woe is me. Everybody has a story, but I feel mine is uniquely scripted. I have a moral and ethical responsibility to effect change in someone else's life, so they don't have to experience what I did. And it's the reason I talk about it.

My father had given me the gun I used when I shot myself. It was a stolen shotgun. He said here, you can have this, and he knew I was struggling in life. Why would you give your kid a shotgun? It's the truth of the matter and he is guilted by it to this day. He justifies giving the gun to me, everybody knows he gave me the gun. The act happened. He has the wrong mindset. Give him a book, give him a Bible, give him money. Don't give him something which will cause destruction. I want the story to be told.

There is hope in the midst of the storm. You're either going through something, or you just came out of something. You matter, and you are not alone.

Conrad Wilson and L.D. Wilson

Larry Wilson's Other Children

In 2016, my dad's brother, Jimmy Daniels attended a barbeque in Kilgore, Texas and he met a woman named Brenda Moss at the party. They chatted and before long, Jimmy and Brenda figured out her birth father was his brother Larry. Jimmy set up a phone call to introduce Brenda and Larry. The first time in her life Brenda talked to her biological father, she was a grown woman.

When my Uncle Jimmy told me about my sister Brenda, it stunned me to find out I had a blood-related sister. No one had ever mentioned her. I struggled during my growing-up years feeling like I didn't belong in the family and now as an adult; I find out I have a sister.

I couldn't wait to meet her. Before I left, I called and told Larry I would be going to Texas to meet my sister. I wasn't asking for permission; I didn't want him to be angry at me for not telling him. When I met Brenda, we immediately formed a special bond. I wanted my father to get acquainted with her, too. I asked Brenda if she wanted to talk to him. She said yes, and we called him. When he answered, I remember being excited "Hey Dad, do you want to talk to your daughter?" and handed Brenda the phone. They only talked for maybe 45 seconds and the call ended. I was so disappointed, I wanted him to give her something, anything. Just this one time, to be a real father.

Brenda suffered from poor health and passed away in 2017 without ever meeting her biological father in person. Larry did not attend her funeral. He chose not to acknowledge her in life and did not respect her in death.

Later in life, Larry had 5 more children with two different women. Two boys and a girl with a white woman named Cathy while he was still married to Mattie. Their names are Chris, Valerie, and Michael.

After he and Mattie divorced, he lived with a woman named Jenny. While in a relationship and living with Jenny, he fathered two more children with another woman. The birth mother ended up in jail for drugs and robbery, and the court sent the two-year-old child to live with Larry and Jenny. After they released her from jail, Larry fathered his second child with the same woman. He was in his 70s when the girls were born. Both girls now live with Larry and Jenny. I admire Jenny and Mattie; they both opened their hearts and homes to children who weren't their own.

Perhaps one day,
they'll understand
all the sacrifices
she gladly made
out of love
for them.

- John Mark Green

CHAPTER FOUR

Mattie Katherine Wilson

My step-mother, Mattie Katherine was born in Lubbock, Texas. Mattie's father died when she was young, and her mother passed when she was 13. Mattie was the oldest of six children and in the sixth grade when she quit school to take care of her brothers and sisters after their mother died. After her mother's death, Mattie needed a family to protect her. A thirteen-year-old girl trying to care for 5 children with no adult present was an easy target.

In those days, black families would 'adopt' orphaned children without legal papers. The children would work in the fields in exchange for a family to care for them. A family adopted Mattie and her brothers and sisters and they moved to Arizona. The children worked side by side with the adoptive family in the cotton fields. The family took care of them and kept them safe.

Mattie married young and had 5 children. When she met Larry Wilson, she and her husband had separated. Larry was an officer in the Air Force, stationed at Luke Air Force Base. He was a basketball player and a smooth talker. Mattie and Larry dated after he returned from California where he had been in a short relationship with my mother, Shirley. When he left California, my mother was pregnant with me.

Ten months after I was born, Mattie and Larry had a baby girl. Larry wanted to name the baby LaSonya. Her name is a mix of Larry + Sonya; La-Sonya. I don't know if Mattie knew my mother's middle name was Sonya. It has never made sense why Larry wanted to name my half-sister after my biological mother.

Larry transferred and moved the family to Salem, Oregon. When they left Arizona, it severed the relationship Mattie's children had with their biological father.

Throughout most of my childhood, Larry did not live with the family. I remember he lived with us for maybe a year before he got his own place. He was not a father figure to any of us. Not to Mattie's children, not to LaSonya, and not to me.

Mattie needed a decent job to support the family since she couldn't count on Larry to help. She enrolled in school. She was raising seven children when she received her high school diploma.

Mattie got a job at the Oregon Women's Correctional Center. She was a hard worker and retired after 25 years as a Recreational Therapist.

I'm not sure how old I was when Larry and Mattie married, but before and after their marriage, he did not live with the family. He lived his own life, leaving Mattie a single mother without the support of a husband. Mattie worked long hours and had a houseful of children to care for. He would fly in and out of our lives when he needed a place to stay or when he came around to stir up trouble.

Occasionally Larry would pick me up to 'spend time with me' and we would go to his current girlfriend's house. They would leave me in the living room to watch television by myself while he and the girlfriend would go into the bedroom and close the door.

My step-mother Mattie was kind and loving. She was the glue holding the family together. She protected me and loved me. She knew I would have a difficult road to travel after my father abducted me. Even with all she did for the family, she could not shield her own children from the dangers of the outside world. Drug and alcohol addiction, gangs, and prison ravaged her family.

Mattie was the neighborhood 'Momma', she opened her home and took in foster children to help with expenses. A steady stream of foster kids came through the house, some paid and some not. Mattie was a conduit in the Salem area for matching black foster children to black families. Growing up as an orphan, she had compassion for children who didn't have a family of their own. I remember times when 15 kids were living in our home.

Mattie wanted to provide a loving home for children who didn't have one. Often in this house full of people, many times no one was paying attention to what was happening behind closed doors. Sadly, due to the lack of attention, a grown man who was a former foster child raped my sister. I was sexually assaulted twice - by a cousin who was babysitting me, and another time by one of the foster kids. I was terrified after it happened.

The abuse is something we've never talked about. Looking back on the traumas we endured, it's no wonder there has been so much pain and heartache in my family.

Mattie passed away in 1998. Family, friends, work colleagues and dignitaries from the state of Oregon attended her funeral. She had touched the lives of so many people, and they all came to pay their respects.

I will always be grateful to Mattie for the love she gave me as a child. She was my Momma. She sheltered me and put herself in danger to protect me from harm. We had a bond of love which can't be broken, I can't wait until I see her again in Heaven.

Mattie Katherine Wilson

Mattie Wilson's Children

Alvin is Mattie's oldest son. He is eleven years older than me, it never seemed like we got to know each other. I felt he was always somewhat distant.

Alvin has epilepsy and suffered grand mal seizures. It was frightening as a young child to see someone lose consciousness, his muscles would tighten, and his body would convulse.

Alvin was a good athlete, and he was a protector. When he married, he and his wife lived in the same house as the extended family. At the time they couldn't afford their own house.

Alvin had two children and he and his wife later divorced. Years after they divorced, my father had a relationship with Alvin's ex-wife.

He still suffers from grand-mal seizures and isn't able to work due to his disability. He remarried and lives in Battleground, Washington.

George was the second of Mattie's children. He was nine years older than me, and he was my favorite. When I was a kid, I adored and looked up to him. George was outgoing, funny, and kind. He was popular in school and was class president his senior year of high school. After graduation, he worked at Nordstrom's, and later as an airline steward.

George and had two children, Charee and George Junior.

Charee's mother was his high school sweetheart. George later dated a woman named Loretta, and she was George Jr.'s mother.

I was with George when he died of aids at age 39.

His sweetheart ended up in prison for drugs. After George died, his brother Gilbert and his wife raised George Jr., he was a 7th or 8th grader at the time of George's death. Her mother and grandmother raised Charee after George died.

George Junior works for a fiberglass warehouse company and has been clean and sober for about 3 years at the time of this writing.

George's daughter, Charee has three boys. She was a drug addict and prostitute and she ended up serving prison time on drug charges. Her father's brother Gilbert and his wife adopted her three children when she went to prison. Someone murdered one of Charee's boys after he got involved with gangs and drugs. She is working hard on turning her life around and she has been clean from drugs for 14 months. Now she is clean and sober and has built relationships with her other two boys.

A tragic loss of a good man, I will always remember him fondly.

George H. 'Teacher George' Bailey

June 4, 1952 — April 22, 1992

George Howard "Teacher George" Bailey, 39, of Salem died Wednesday.

He was born in Glendale, Ariz., and graduated from North Salem High School. He later attended Willamette and Arizona State universities.

He worked for United Airlines for 18 years as an international representative for Inflight Services.

He enjoyed traveling and working with youth. He was also a dedicated worker for Salem Mission Church of God in Christ.

He is survived by his daughter, Charee Bailey of Portland; son, George H. Jr. of Salem; mother, Missionary Mattie K. Wilson of Salem; stepfather, Larry D. Wilson of Salem; sisters, Regina K. Germany and Lasonya Sedore both of Salem, and Sandra and Nakalia Bailey both of Phoenix, Ariz.; brothers, Alvin and Gary L. both of Portland, Gilbert C. of Salem, Larry C. Wilson Jr. of Gresham, and Terry, Richard and Austin Bailey all of Phoenix; grandfather, George H. Henderson of Phoenix; and three grandchildren.

Visiting will be from 1 to 6 p.m. Saturday and from 10 a.m. to 6 p.m. Sunday in Virgil T. Golden mortuary. Funeral services will begin at 1 p.m. Monday in the church. Interment will be at City View Cemetery.

George Bailey Obituary

Gary was 7 years older than me. He was a phenomenal athlete. He played basketball and football in high school and in college at Southern Oregon University. Gary's high school team won the Oregon state championship in 1971.

Gary was another child in the family with a drug problem. He spent one month in the county jail on drug charges and then turned his life around. He graduated from college worked as a manager at Tektronix until his retirement.

Gary has 2 daughters. He found out his wife was gay 10 years into their marriage. They stayed together and raised the girls until they graduated college and then divorced and went their separate ways. Gary is now enjoying his retirement.

Gilbert is 3 years older than I am. Gilbert has a heart condition, and he was never really in good health. We were not close because of the sibling rivalry between us. Gilbert made me feel like I didn't belong in the family. He was mean growing up, and as an adult, he hasn't gotten over his resentment toward me.

When Mattie died, Gilbert told me, "get with your own blood" implying I should end my relationships with Mattie's children and stay away from the family. He never understood or acknowledged this family was the only family I have ever known.

Gilbert and his wife Kathy had three children of their own. They adopted George Jr. when George died and adopted Charee's three boys when she went to prison. They raised those eight children and later became foster parents for

MMRD (Mentally Retarded or Special Needs) Sex Offenders.

Gilbert and Kathy's son Craig was born with Down Syndrome. Craig's severe physical disabilities left him confined to a wheelchair. Craig died in 2016 at the age of 37. When I learned Craig had passed, I called Gilbert to tell him how sorry I was. I wanted to attend the funeral, but Gilbert said he didn't want me there and hung up.

I wasn't sure if I should show up at the funeral, I knew he was grieving, and I wanted to pay my respects. I called my father, and he said: "just don't go, we don't want no trouble at the funeral." I felt terrible but decided it was best not to go. I didn't want to cause more hard feelings between Gilbert and myself.

Gilbert and I have not talked for 7 years now other than the phone call after his son Craig died.

Regina was older than me. She was pregnant when she was just 14. The father was Curtis Williams, one of the foster kids. He was in his late 20's when Regina became pregnant. He had no business having a relationship with her, she was a vulnerable child. Regina dropped out of school in the eighth grade when she had the baby, a child raising a child. Mattie and the rest of the household helped Regina raise the daughter she named Crystal.

Curtis Williams did not play any role in Crystal's life growing up. He was an alcoholic and a drug addict. His health suffered due to his addictions, and he died in Arizona in the early 2000's.

Five years after Crystal was born, Regina had a son named Michael. Michael was about 9 years old when his father was murdered; shot multiple times as he was coming out of a nightclub. They called him Little Joe Bell.

Michael got involved in a gang and drugs. He is currently serving a 30-year prison sentence at Oregon State Penitentiary for drugs and robbery. He was incarcerated when I worked at the prison.

Crystal served time at the Coffee Creek prison on drug charges and released in 2016. She has a pacemaker because of heart damage due to drug use.

Regina has another daughter, her name is Mattie, she lives in Denver and has 2 children.

Life has not been kind to Regina. She's a long-time drug addict - Meth and Crack are her drugs of choice. In 2015, I visited Regina in Denver and saw firsthand how addiction has a hold on her. She openly smoked Meth in front of me many times while I was there. It truly made me sad to see her like that, I remember when she was a vibrant, beautiful young woman.

LaSonya was the only one of Mattie's children I was related to by blood. LaSonya is also a recovering addict. When her son George Jr. was born, he was a crack baby. He was taken away from LaSonya by the State of Oregon. My wife and I petitioned the State, and we were able to take him in and care for him for a year while LaSonya served her sentence. After she got clean, she had another child, and named her LaMattie. She was 4 years younger than George Jr.

LaSonya cleaned up her life and now she's following in Mattie's footsteps. She has two children of her own and six foster children. LaSonya nurtured four foster kids through their high school years. She runs a group home in Salem now. We call her Little Katherine, she looks like Mattie and has a heart for children.

There is
so much
bad
in the world,
keep doing good
and make a
difference.

- Conrad Wilson

CHAPTER FIVE

Foster Children

My stepmother Mattie was a caring and loving woman who opened her home to many foster children throughout the years. She found services for the children, provided a hot meal, a place to sleep and a roof over their heads. With many of the kids she fostered, she didn't receive compensation; she took them in because they needed a home.

Some children came to us because Mattie had known their parents. One boy named Robert arrived after his father died. Other children were removed from abusive situations. Sometimes neighborhood kids who had nowhere to go would come and sleep on the floor. Mattie treated the children as if they were her own.

Having foster kids in the home was difficult. If you weren't first to the table or didn't grab your plate, there might not be enough food for everyone. Mattie would put away food for those who came in late, but it wasn't a guarantee you would get to eat. I learned to hoard food and to hide food for later. Those were difficult times.

As a child, I was challenged by all the people she took in, I didn't quite understand it. As I matured, I could see her gracious and unconditional love, and it brought me to the full knowledge of why she did it. She was a product of a foster adoption, and I think bringing in these children was her way of giving back.

It forged my mission in life, which is helping people get where they need to be - regardless of where they come from. She ingrained it in me.

I suffered from being abused and Mattie had no knowledge it had happened. I was sexually abused by someone she trusted to babysit me in her absence. I didn't have the heart to tell her, or the courage. Again, there's no blame coming when there are 9 or 10 different people besides her own five children living there including myself. You're just grateful to have someone showing you some love and affection.

Our home was chaotic. There was abuse, both emotional and physical. There was a pecking order like in a normal family. I was the youngest at the time and I was the ugly duckling. The other children in the family had darker skin than I did. I'm Puerto Rican and African-American, and everyone else was one hundred percent African-American, and they all had darker skin.

We played with the white kids in the neighborhood and with the foster brothers and sisters. We had a rainbow, it was cool. Now I look at it as an adult and I can see it from a different perspective. I think it's why I was a good father because she set these foundational principles. I raised my children with those same principles. I would never have foster children because I didn't want to subject my own children to what I grew up with, but the foundational principles were like anything else you learn and grow from. Yes, it was quite difficult but again; it was a blessing in disguise.

I have a mother who was my birth mother, but I also have a Momma, and Mattie Wilson was my Momma. It's how I reference her, she was my Momma. The foster children were one of the best things to happen in hindsight, even the abuse.

When you're in the middle of something you might not see the blessings, or the things which aren't blessings. With so many children in the house, not knowing who was coming and going, and how many people would be there at any given time, it was a survival situation for a little boy.

My father was in and out as far as living in the home with the family and Mattie and the biological children. Much of the time when I was growing up, he lived somewhere else. My father was from East Texas, he joined the military to get away. We migrated to Oregon, and he became a serious alcoholic and a very abusive person.

He never told me he loved me until I was 30 years old, I grew up thinking he didn't love me. He was never there.

He was friends with the foster brothers; most of them were about 10 years older than me. He partied with them, and he drank with them. He had girlfriends on the side, and I'm sure they were part of the party scene, too.

I remember specifically a barbecue at our house. One of the former foster brothers was now in his 30s, and he was there. His name was Cornell Garrett. He and my father got into an argument, my father had one arm at the time (I don't remember him with two arms). The guy shoved my father up against the wall of the house and this incident lead into a shooting.

My father ran into the house, everyone was still outside drinking and barbecuing. There were many people there. My father runs out of the house with a gun. Cornell was in his car and my dad had a big gun, it was a 357 magnum. He stood on the street corner and he emptied the gun into the car.

Bullets flew into the front window of the neighbor's house. One bullet hit Cornell, and he laid down in the car. My father emptied the other bullets into the car. We're talking big holes, two inches in diameter. It hit Cornell in the stomach. My father went back to the house and the former foster kid drove off.

The police and the ambulance came. My father turned himself in about eight hours later and got bailed out of jail. The former foster kid would not testify against my father and my father ended up not being charged with a crime.

To this day, Cornell and my father are friends but they're not close. He doesn't consider him to be one of his sons; he considers him an acquaintance. The other foster kids consider Cornell a brother, and I do too. Years later when Mattie passed away, Cornell came to her funeral to pay his respects.

> In other cases, Larry Darnell Wilson, 39, 2102 4th St. NE, pleaded innocent to charges of assault and being a convicted felon in possession of a firearm. He was charged following an argument with Cornell Garrett Jr., 24, 6453 Ruggles Ave. S, on May 24 outside Wilson's home, authorities said. Garrett jumped in his car and as he was backing out into the street, he was hit through the windshield by several pistol shots, they added. Garrett was treated and released from Salem Hospital for a chest wound.

Oregon Statesman, June 4, 1975

My father was a ruthless guy if you crossed him, he'd kill you. And he tried to kill this guy. It's been at least 30 years since the event, but I remember like it happened yesterday. I've had dreams and flashbacks about it throughout my life. There was never any debrief or explanation about why this went down. We had to fend for ourselves to figure out what had happened. You asked the other kids, and those were the stories you grew up with.

When arguments would break out, he would just jump out with a gun. My dad was a gangster Bonnie and Clyde type of guy. Just being real. Now I'm a mature adult I can see it, and he's finally calmed down. He's 83 years old and has signs of dementia.

I still don't trust him, and I will never trust him. He keeps a gun right in his living room, it's the way he grew up. I never wanted to make him mad. I've had him get mad at me since then and I had to leave because I thought he might shoot me.

All the kids believe to this day if you crossed him you were in danger. This is what he did to a foster child. Everyone's moved on with their life, but Larry Wilson Sr. is not someone you would want to cross.

It was a horrible situation, but the foster kids still respected him and if something happened to one of them, he would be there. It was weird how the dynamic worked, how a kid who's been abused wants to go back to the abusive parents. In his own way, he showed the kids love, and he gave them a better life than they would have had otherwise.

The foster boys were young enough they were like friends more than father and sons. There were kids younger than me, but he treated them all like they were buddies. They did whatever the boys do together, it was always chaotic.

I remember him shooting the ceiling when he got in a fight with my Momma. I remember her hovering over me to protect me after he had slapped me upside the head. Once when he came over and the dog dish was empty, he immediately slapped me before anyone could tell him I had already fed the dog. The bowl was empty because the dog had eaten the food. He slapped me off my chair. He had this thing like a razor strap on the wall and would use it to beat me; she hovered over me and he beat her instead and I did not get hit.

The foster dad, the crazy dad who brutalized his kids was Larry Wilson. I love him, and the Bible says to honor your mother and father and your days will be long in the land, so I honor him. He taught me what I do not want to be and that's the bottom line.

I love him I don't trust him

I told myself I would break this generational curse for my own kids, and I did. And he taught me I didn't want to be like him. Mattie was the rock for everyone, she protected us and she fought him back. I remember her sticking him with an ice pick in front of all of us. I've seen her dig him a couple of times, blood flying and everything. He had to know he could not walk over her. She is the one woman to this day he loved like nobody's business because she would stand up against him. And she stood up for us. It's fresh in my memory like it happened yesterday.

The foster kids grew up and moved on. Over the years a few have died. Some of them ended up in prison and some are still in my life. Whether it's nearby or across the United States, we've remained friends. Mattie treated the children as if they were her own.

I became the man I am because of Mattie Wilson. She played an intricate role in my life. She stepped in to become a mother to me when I had been taken away from my birth mother. She was the only mother I knew until I was in my twenties.

She took in those foster children and still provided the love and support I needed as a young boy growing up. The impact those foster kids had on me-the good, the bad, and the ugly outweighed anything which could have set me back.

I have a true love for her and a sincere love for my foster brothers and sisters who are still a part of my life. The journey was a blessing in disguise.

Trauma

/troumə,trômə/

The response to a deeply distressing or disturbing event that overwhelms an individual's ability to cope

CHAPTER SIX

Growing Up

As a very young child, I lived in Los Angeles with my mother. When I was 18 months old, my father came to our house and said he was taking me out for ice cream. He picked me up and never took me home.

At the time he abducted me, it was before missing children's faces were displayed on milk cartons, before AMBER Alerts. My mother was a minority woman living in Los Angeles in the 1960s. A single parent who didn't have the resources available to find me. She must have been out of her mind with worry.

My given name is Conrad. After he kidnapped me, my father started calling me Larry. He knew my mother would not be looking for a child named Larry Wilson. I didn't know he kidnapped me; I was so young. I never wrapped my head around it until I was an adult.

My father has never talked about my mother and the circumstances around taking me from her.

When my father picked me up, we drove from Los Angeles to Arizona. I became part of a blended family; my father, his girlfriend Mattie and her 6 children. My father and Mattie later married.

My father was distant, and he was gone quite often. He didn't try to build a relationship with me after kidnapping me. I believe he took me to hurt my mother.

My stepmother Mattie Katherine knew it was hard for me being an only child who was taken from everything familiar and thrust into a large family. She made me feel like I belonged.

My new brothers and sisters were typical kids. There were times I felt accepted as a brother, and many times when I didn't.

We left Arizona and moved to Salem. It wasn't a diverse community and there were many unresolved racial issues. In 1968, during the heat of the civil rights movement, my family was the target of many incidents which now we appropriately call hate crimes. People in the community who didn't want a black family there intimidated and harassed us.

One of the most horrific incidents happened on May 10, 1968. It was around 2:30 a.m. when a vehicle with a loud muffler drove down our street. Suddenly, shots rang out. Someone fired ten shots, two of the bullets went into the bedroom where my step-brother and I were sleeping.

After hearing the gunshots, my father ran outside into the street. By the time he got outside, the car was gone.

There hadn't been drive-by shootings on the West Coast since the Martin Luther King Jr. assassination. This was the first drive-by shooting in the Pacific Northwest.

We were sleeping peacefully in our home. My family – me, my father, his wife, and my brothers and sisters could have been killed. No one was hurt in the shooting, but it terrified me. It was a very traumatic time for our family; we had done nothing wrong.

I was in Kindergarten when the shooting happened. It was in the paper, and everyone knew about it. We were fortunate, there were people who rallied around us and were protective of the children in the family. We received counseling services, food, and community support.

Police Chief Ben H. Meyers promised a complete investigation, but there were no positive leads. Detectives investigated the crime scene and gathered the physical evidence. They recovered ten bullets, from two guns; a .22 caliber and a .25 caliber. It was obvious the intention was to harm us.

The Salem Area Human Relations Commission reviewed the police report. The processing of the crime scene and protection for the family received an unsatisfactory rating. The scientific work received a positive rating. There were still many unresolved questions.

After they released the police report, we learned the police department had not been sending hourly patrols to our house as they had promised. Finally, a detective was assigned to check in on us daily for our safety.

We had moved from Arizona to Oregon in search of a better life and to live in a safe community. The torment of our family did not take place where the civil rights movement was active, it was in the small town of Salem, Oregon–far away from the unrest in other parts of the country.

My family should have felt safe in our home and in our neighborhood.

2 Sleeping Children Almost Hit in Attack on Negro Home

(Story, picture also on page 1.)

One of the score of bullets fired into a Negro family's home here early Friday just missed two sleeping children.

Police were called to the Larry D. Wilson home at 1605 4th St. NE, about 2:30 a.m. when about 10 bullets, apparently from a small caliber automatic weapon, were fired into the Wilson home.

One of three shots which ripped through a south wall and window passed six inches above the mattress where Gilbert, 10, and Larry, 7, were sleeping in a double bed. It apparently passed between the two heads. Seven other shots struck the east side of the house, one just above three other sleeping children, Lasonya, 6, and John, who was 2 years old Friday.

Three at Home

In the home at the time of the shooting were Mr. and Mrs. Wilson, A. D. Bailey, 18, her oldest son by a previous marriage, his wife Gloria, 18; George, 16; Gary, 14; Regina, 12; Gilbert, 10; Larry, 7; Lasonya, 6 and John, 2; and a friend Herman Andino, 23, who is staying with the family.

Mrs. Wilson said she and her husband awoke to the sound of gunshots and a speeding car. Three shots hit the front upstairs section and seven others fired at the east side of the home as the car turned left off Norway and sped north on 4th Street. It was described as a late model auto with a loud muffler.

Mr. Wilson got up and ran toward the outside, saying, "I'm going to shoot it," Mrs. Wilson said later.

"I wonder who would do a thing like that, but they sure did."

Except for John, who slept through the shooting, others in the home remained awake the rest of the morning.

"We couldn't very well go back to sleep when someone shoots in your home at 2:30 in the morning," said Mrs. Wilson, who suddenly remembered it was John's 2nd birthday. Picking him up, she said, "you didn't wake up did you?" John responded with a big grin.

5 Slugs Found

Officers recovered five bullets that appeared to be from a .22 caliber long casing, or possibly a little larger .25 caliber, they said.

All the shots were fired into the upstairs section of the home, perhaps aimed high to clear parked autos. Several pierced

Principal Takes Post at Marquam

Statesman News Service

SILVERTON — Bradley Jefferies, Silverton, has accepted a position as principal of Butte Creek School at Marquam for this fall.

Jeffries is a graduate of Silverton High School and Mount Angel College and has been principal of St. Paul's Elementary School for the past five years.

Carnival Plays At Legion Site

A fund-raising carnival sponsored by American Legion Capitol Post 9 continues today and Sunday at Post headquarters, 4025 Commercial St. SE.

The show features Blake & Son's carnival rides, games and other amusements. It runs from 11 a.m. to midnight today, and noon until 11 p.m. Sunday.

Proceeds will help develop a sports facility for youth.

Cook to Retire

TURNER — Retiring after nearly 17 years as cook at Turner Elementary School is Mrs. Julia Ann Harrington, Turner. Before moving to Turner, Mrs. Harington was cook at Oregon State Tuberculosis Hospital.

Cacao may have originated in Brazil.

windows, others lodged in exterior and interior walls.

Uniformed patrols searched the area and detectives arrived later to begin an examination of physical evidence, including a search for bullets that will be sent to the State Police Crime Laboratory for ballistics examination.

Chief Ben H. Meyers promised a complete investigation. But he said the department has no positive leads.

The family had been the target of some racial incidents about 18 months ago.

In 1966, crosses were placed in the yard and porch and at an earlier residence at Court and 17th Streets NE. An apple throwing incident in 1968 broke a window and one of the Wilson children recived a minor cut.

Oregon Statesman, May 11, 1968

Shots Riddle Salem Home

Oregon Statesman, May 11, 1968

Minister Asks Tips On Shooting

Police continued to investigate over the weekend an early Friday incident in which the home of a North Salem Negro family was riddled with bullets. About 10 shots, apparently fired from a fast-moving auto, struck the home of Larry D. Wilson, 1605 4th St. NE., about 2:30 a.m.

Saturday the Rev. Henry L. Haines, president of the Salem Area Human Relations Commission, issued a statement calling . . . "upon any citizen having information that would assist in apprehending the person or persons who fired bullets into" . . . the residence and asked that they "come forward with that evidence."

"I call upon citizens of the Salem area to demonstrate in some positive way their outrage against this attack upon human life and to express their desire that the Larry Wilson family not only be allowed to live in peace but also be warmly welcomed into this community."

"We can reduce the possibility of such inhuman and lawless acts in the future if we will openly reject racism and accept our common humanity," the Rev. Haines said.

Oregon Statesman, May 12, 1968

Report Is Critical of Police In Shootup of Negro Home

By ALLEN J. MORRISON
Staff Writer, The Statesman

A special committee of the Salem Area Human Relations Commission presented a report Tuesday night that contained some direct or implied criticism of the city police department's handling of a case in which a Negro family's home

Westmoreland Asks More GIs

MANILA (AP) — Gen. William C. Westmoreland, former commander of U.S. forces in Vietnam, urged Tuesday more American troops for the Vietnam war.

Westmoreland called for an additional troop buildup of 15,000 men to support the present 535,000 U.S. fighting men now on the war front.

The four-star general said, however, the United States can reduce its level of commitments, possibly in troops in 18 months "if South Vietnam can bear a greater load of the fighting."

; Battle

was riddled with bullets May 16.

Police Chief Benjamin H. Meyers, a member of the commission, vocally defended the police investigation of the shooting and said the report contained some untruths or statements taken out of context.

Prompted by Complaint

The issue arose at the commission's May 22 meeting after

CBS to Reduce Violence on TV

NEW YORK (AP) — The Columbia Broadcasting System said Tuesday it has begun steps to "de-emphasize violence in programs now in production."

Dr. Frank Stanton, president of CBS, said the network shared President Johnson's concern "as to the possible effect of the content of television entertainment programs upon the nature of our society."

Dr. Stanton warned, however, that "it may take a considerable length of time to determine whether there is a causal relationship between the fictional portrayal of violence in the mass media and any increase of actual violence in American life. Nevertheless, we are re-examining our policies and practices in this entire area."

member James Berry questioned whether the Larry D. Wilson family at 1605 4th St. NE, were receiving adequate police protection following the shooting at their home, where one of 11 shots fired barely missed two sleeping children.

Capt. Glenn Bowman answered that police were patrolling the home more than once an hour. At that point the commission appointed Berry, an insuranceman, and Robert L. Stevens, manager of the State Fair to talk with city officials, police and anyone else with knowledge of the case and to submit a report.

"Started Later"

Berry and Stevens' report indicated that police initiated hourly patrols by the Wilson home following their discussion of the case with police, some two weeks after the shooting.

Chief Meyers denied this. He said the family was getting hourly patrols but in the presence of Stevens, Berry and other police that he reiterated a command to Capt. Bowman to make sure the Wilson family notices the patrols by shining a spot light on the window.

The chief said the department had been attempting to keep the surveillance under cover in the hopes of catching those allegedly harrassing the family.

(Additional details on pages 2 and 6.)

Oregon Statesman, June 12, 1968

Sleepless Nights

The harassment and intimidation continued. People drove past our home throwing trash and dead animal carcasses in our yard. We had many sleepless nights, it wasn't a pleasant way to live.

On May 15, 1968, my father received an anonymous letter demanding we leave town. He immediately left to file a police report. Before leaving the police station, my father assured them we were not leaving town. He said to them, "I have been running for years, and every place is no different. I might die, but I'm not leaving."

People in the community embraced our family. The Bailey family helped us move from our home in North East Salem to a home in South Salem. The new house was across the street from the home of the Secretary of State, Clay Myers. Our family had a new sense of security and we felt safe again.

Letter Tells Negro to Quit City

By JOE MORTON
Staff Writer, The Statesman

Larry D. Wilson, Salem Negro whose home was riddled with bullets last Friday morning, received a letter Wednesday demanding he get out of town.

Wilson, a one-armed cement finisher for Salem Public Works Department, stopped by The Statesman long enough for the type-written note to be copied, then hurried off to Salem police department saying he hoped they could find out who sent it.

"You must know how it would be. I don't know what to think," he said when asked if he suspected the note came from the same people who shot up his house.

The letter was postmarked in McMinnville.

"I'll tell you one thing. I'm

Two Brothers Face Charge

Statesman News Service

DALLAS — Two Salem brothers were arrested Wednesday on charges of assault with intent to rob on the complaint of a Dallas man.

Jerry L. Stewart, 23, and

not leaving town. I'll die here if I must," he said.

He said he had to hurry to the police station so he could get right back home. "I s u r e don't want anything to happen while I'm gone," he said. "It's getting pretty hard working day and staying up nights in case something else happens."

One of about 10 shots from .22 caliber weapon barely missed the heads of two children sleeping in a double bed. The incident occurred about 2:30 a.m.

Police are still investigating the shooting, but report no positive leads.

Oregon Statesman, May 16, 1968

Push yourself
again and again.

Don't give an inch
until
the final buzzer
sounds.

- Larry Bird

CHAPTER SEVEN

Basketball

I spent long hours shooting hoops in the driveway. I was the smallest kid in the family and I learned to shoot from the outside. I quickly found out I didn't have to fight for a shot from the inside against kids who were bigger than me.

In high school, I knew athletics would be the way to get out of my situation at home and become successful at something I enjoyed. Basketball quickly became my coping skill. I didn't feel loved or accepted at home, but when I scored points in the game, the crowd would yell my name and applaud me. I interpreted their enthusiasm as love, so I played harder to score more points.

I broke the Junior High City Scoring Record, making 19 of 22 shots, and scoring 38 points without going to the free throw line. There was an article in the paper and people were taking notice.

In my Junior year at McNary High School, I lead the Valley in scoring. I was one of three top scoring leaders in the State. While still in High School, I practiced with Willamette University's men's basketball team. I practiced with the team for two years.

In April 1979, I received a letter from the National High School Athletic Association. The players selected are the 'cream of the crop' for lack of a better term. The high school All-Star games are an opportunity for college coaches from around the country to watch athletes from different parts of the United States. I played in the game even though I had already signed a letter of intent with the University of Detroit Titans.

I met retired Oregon State Congressman and high school basketball coach Victor Backlund when I attended McNary High School. During my sophomore year, the local paper interviewed Backlund, and he said "Larry (Conrad) is living proof good things do indeed come in small packages. He is the smallest player in the Valley League at 5'8" and 135 pounds."

I worked hard to improve my game. I set the city game scoring record, with a 38-point performance, hitting 19 of 22 shots from the floor. My overall ball handling skills and speed was setting me apart, and I was getting noticed.

A collective group of coaches said there was no doubt I was one of the most exciting performers in the league in years. In one of our media interviews, Backland said "This was one of the best decisions I have ever made. Larry (Conrad) has become an outstanding basketball player."

I had my weaknesses, too. I struggled to control my emotions on the court. I became angry and frustrated over small things. I would let nonsense like a missed shot bother me too much.

My coach didn't know the full story of what was happening at home. He didn't know I hadn't seen my mother in years and no one would talk about her and I didn't know the reason why. He didn't know my father was abusive, distant, and absent most of the time. He didn't know I was just trying to survive my high school years in a family where I often felt alone and like I didn't fit in.

People could see my potential, and they could see my anger. I didn't talk to people about my home situation. I tried to appear happy on the outside, but the anger was there - just under the surface. When I was younger, my anger was a detriment. As I matured, I learned to direct the anger by focusing on the passion I had for the game.

My father did not support me when I played ball. He didn't practice with me and he did not attend my games. On Senior Night, the player's mothers were honored. Mattie was there to support me. At half-time the mothers were called down to the court. The cheerleading squad gave each mother a bouquet of roses to thank them for their support over the years. I was happy and proud having Mattie there for me.

My happiness turned to horror when out of nowhere, my father came onto the court, grabbing me by the elbow and pulling me off the court. He was drunk and yelling at me "get off the court, we don't need this". He was furious they were honoring Mattie for being my 'mom' in front of the crowd. I could not believe what was happening. I tried for so long to keep this part of my life hidden, but there he was - embarrassing me in a drunken tirade in front of not only my coach and team, but the whole town.

My coaches tried to get him off the court, but he wouldn't let go of me and was yelling profanities and trying to drag me with him. The police had to intervene; they removed him from the gym and arrested him. This embarrassing scene happened at half-time, I had to go back and play the second half of the game after being publicly humiliated by someone who should have been there supporting me.

I was recruited by the top Division One basketball programs in the country. The most notable was by popular ESPN analyst Dick Vitale. At the time he was the head basketball coach at The University of Detroit Michigan. I took a trip with my mother Mattie, to visit the University of Detroit and Coach Vitale.

I liked what I heard about the program and made a verbal commitment. When I went back for a second visit during spring training, I had more time to look around. I felt lonely, and a long way from home. The school was in a deteriorated area, nothing like where I grew up in California, Arizona, and Oregon. I decided this wasn't where I wanted to spend my college career. I came back to Oregon and told my mother I didn't want to be so far away from home. I looked into the other colleges who had recruited me before I left for Detroit.

Oregon Statesman

After graduating High School, I went to California for the summer. I spent my time playing basketball in the parks of Los Angeles. Darby Park, Will Rogers Park, Centinella Park, and Fox Hill Park. The Los Angeles Forum was just up the street from Darby park. NBA players would come to the parks in the off-season and work out. Magic Johnson played at Darby Park in the summer months. Raymond Lewis who had been blackballed from the NBA took his game to those courts and ended up playing in the European league. What an amazing time for a kid from Salem Oregon to be in Los Angeles, playing ball with my heroes.

When I was in Los Angeles, I rekindled the relationship with Robin, my childhood sweetheart. I stayed over for the summer with Robin at her mother's house.

I visited Stanford University. I knew I wasn't academically sharp enough to go there, but they said they would make concessions. Since I had made the verbal commitment to Detroit, I had to sit out for a year before I could play basketball with any other school.

I was homesick; I was a momma's boy, and I didn't want to be far from home. I returned to Oregon and met with Glenn Kenny from Portland State University and he offered me a full ride scholarship. Glenn was the head basketball coach for the Portland State Vikings and they had recently recruited Freeman Williams. Freeman Williams came from Los Angeles and was three years ahead of me in school. He had broken a scoring record at Portland State, scoring 71 points in a single game and they used it to leverage me to play there. I signed a letter of intent.

I was a confused young man. I ended up walking away from the full-ride scholarship to go to California and be with my girlfriend. I didn't have much parental guidance, and with no father figure in my life I didn't know what I should do. I went back to West Los Angeles College in Culver City, California so I could be close to the girl I was in love with. Going back to Los Angeles led me to Cal-State Dominguez Hills. I tried out and made the team. I played there for a year and ended up injured, with a torn meniscus. When I went back to Oregon to recover from my injury, Robin called me to share the news I would be a father. I won't forget the moment I had to make a life-changing and difficult decision, to pursue my lifelong childhood dream of becoming a professional NBA player or to become a responsible father. I chose Plan B, and now over twenty years later, I continue to appreciate the blessing of choosing my child over my pride.

When we moved back to Oregon, I attended Chemeketa Junior College. Rick Adelman, an ex-NBA player and coach for the Portland Trail Blazers, had taken a sabbatical from the Blazers and was coaching at Chemeketa. With a record of 28-0, we won the national title against a team out of Texas; they had a famous player by the name of Spud Webb on the team.

When I left Chemeketa, I had two years of eligibility left, and I was offered a scholarship to play at Syracuse University. Jimmy Boeheim was the head coach at Syracuse. I never played in my time there. I was a red-shirt junior, and I didn't get a starting spot. I stayed there trying to figure out what to do with my life. I had a family to support, and I needed to make some important decisions.

I looked into going abroad to play basketball and tried out for a team overseas, but it didn't work out. I kept trying to create income. I came back to Oregon and played at Western Baptist College for Coach Tim Hills for two years. The school later changed the name to Corban University.

I knew I had the talent, but I wasn't in the right place. I stayed connected with different professional athletes. I traveled to Brazil and played on the International team there for a year. After Brazil, I went to Mexico and played for a year. I thought playing internationally wasn't getting me anywhere. The travel wore on me, my son was growing, and my wife and son were in the States while I was out of the country.

The Houston Rockets invited me to try out. Through hard work and obedience, I began my basketball career in the official NBA Development League playing for the Rio Renegades. The Development League was a stepping stone to the NBA, preparing players, coaches, and officials for the NBA. By this time, I'm an older guy and I'm maturing. I have a wife and a son to support, and we wanted another child.

I decided it was time to look for work outside of basketball, and I accepted a position in an adult maximum-security prison. I worked as a Recreational Therapist and then as the Activities Director at the Oregon State Correctional Institution. I volunteered in my local community as a basketball coach and mentor. In my spare time, I continued to work on my game.

I found my passion in mentoring troubled youth. I transferred to the Oregon Youth Authority Correctional Facility. I gained valuable experience working as a counselor, learning to understand and connect with young people.

I moved into field work as a Juvenile Parole and Probation Officer. My territory covered all counties in the State of Oregon. I worked in partnership with community treatment programs to help troubled kids become productive citizens and acclimate back into the community.

I was offered a job as the Shooting and Player Development Coach in Minnesota. I was in Minnesota for two years under head coach Rick Adelman. When Rick Adelman retired, and Kevin McHale moved to Houston, I moved to Houston, too.

I've been around the league and learned the ins and outs as a player and a coach. I was in contract with the NBA team in Houston, Texas when I landed a contract with the NBA team in Phoenix, Arizona. I work as a player development coach and an international sports recruiter. My specialty is recruiting athletes for college teams. I'm still working and involved in sports

Statesman-Journal file photo

WARRIORS' LEADER — Larry Wilson, a former McNary High athlete who played for Chemeketa Community College last season, is expected to be the court leader for Western Baptist this season.

Oregon Statesman

WB's Wilson no longer has chip on shoulder

By DEBBIE HOWLETT
Of the Statesman-Journal

"You know, in high school I was having an identity crisis. I was labeled an offensive machine. It was a lot of fame and fortune. It really can make your head swell."

— Larry Wilson

His basketball skills are mostly offensive. Up until a couple of years ago, so was Larry Wilson.

"He used to have a terrible attitude," said Tim Collins, who met Wilson when he was a freshman at McNary High and now coaches him at Western Baptist College. "He was self-centered. He ran around with a chip on his shoulder."

The chip is gone and, in Wilson's words, "the burden is lighter."

What happened to Wilson after he left McNary in 1980, a year when he was named all-state and and a year after he led the Valley League in scoring?

Wilson thought college, thanks to a full scholarship, was the answer. But he stumbled at Portland State. He decided the Vikings' program wasn't what he wanted.

"At the time my head was still growing," Wilson said.

He transferred to Cal State-Dominguez Hills, where he found little in the way of basketball, plenty in the way of grief.

"What I was doing was kind of running away from reality," Wilson said. "I never drank or messed with any drugs, I was just kind of a cocky kid."

It was in Dominguez Hills, just outside of Los Angeles, where Wilson decided to go about his business

— without basketball. Enrolling in junior college classes and working at a variety of jobs, Wilson gradually changed.

He married. He and his wife Robin had a son Bryson, now three. And Wilson turned to religion.

"That has made the sole difference in my life," Wilson said. "I was looking for direction. Nothing really went wrong or had, it was just a missing link. It's just given me a clear handle."

Robin Wilson encouraged her husband to try basketball again. It was all he needed.

The next year Wilson enrolled at Chemeketa Community College and played basketball under the direction of Rick Adelman, now an assistant with the Portland Trail Blazers.

It was a tough year, though.

"I sat (the bench) the whole year knowing that I could start," Wilson said. "The most I ever played was three minutes against some JV team. The old Larry Wilson would have quit."

The old Larry Wilson is someone the new Larry Wilson doesn't like very much.

"You know, in high school I was having an identity crisis," he said.

"I was labeled an offensive machine. It was a lot of fame and fortune. It really can make your head swell, I don't like to look back on the past, it throws you off."

But Wilson remembers the beginning. He even remembers the numbers.

"It started in junior high," he said. "I scored 38 points in one game, 19 of 22, and it made a lot of difference. People paid attention.

"It came just a little too easy."

It was the same thing in high school. Wilson was known for his basketball talents and little else.

"Now there's more to life than playing basketball," he said.

Wilson is thriving at Western Baptist. He lives off campus, but spends most of the day at the school.

He said he's happier at the small, conservative christian college with a student body of about 250 than any place else he's been.

Collins is glad to have Wilson on the basketball team, and Wilson is glad to be there. He's the first man off the bench and likes that role, even to the point of requesting that Collins not start him ahead of a senior, whom Wilson said deserves the job more than he.

But the students, who chant

"Larry, Larry," during games, appreciate him as much for his lifestyle as his athletic abilities.

Wilson has found it in himself to adjust to Western Baptist's philosophy, including a dress code and a hair cut code in addition to daily chapel services.

"We want to create an image that is acceptable to all people. Disneyland has the same thing," Collins said. "He cut his hair — he used to look like Lionel Ritchie. He was so willing to make those changes, which again is not very much like Larry before."

Wilson is aware that his basketball talents have brought him much of what he has, but said that his turn to religion and a christian school are just as important.

"His ability to take his mind off himself has been a real turnaround in his life," Collins said. "It's a carry-over to basketball."

After basketball is over with, Wilson said he'd like his new-found faith to carry over to his professional life.

If basketball after graduation isn't in the cards, he'd like to work with young people, possibly as a counselor, or just as someone to look up to.

"I had a lot of idols, but they were far away," Wilson said. "One of my goals is just to be able to deal with youth."

It seems like he's already accomplished that much.

Oregon Statesman, Jan 24, 1985

Some people come
into our lives and
quickly go. Some
stay for a while and
leave footprints on
our hearts and we
are never the same.

- C.C. Scott

CHAPTER EIGHT

My Family

I met Robin picking strawberries in the summer months of junior high school. She was working on a snack truck owned by her grandparents, selling food and snacks to the people working in the fields. This was right outside of Salem in the small farm town of Independence Oregon. Robin moved back and forth to Los Angeles where her mom and dad lived. She often came back in the summer to visit her grandparents. The summer of my senior year she came back to Oregon, and I fell for her. I walked away from a full scholarship at a major university to pursue her and my college experience in the huge City of Los Angeles.

While is Los Angeles, I was injured playing basketball and had gone back to Oregon to recover. Robin called to tell me she was pregnant, and we moved to Oregon and had our first child. My son Bryson, a precious gift from

God. I had to make tough decisions, and I wanted to be a better father than the father my dad was, so I pursued my hoop career with a family. Some doors closed, and others opened. Keeping my family intact was the best decision I have ever made in life, aside from giving my life to Christ.

Robin and I were together for twenty-two years. Robin was the best thing to happen to me. I don't know how she dealt with the tragic situation of the shooting, but she did. She checked out emotionally, which is understandable in hindsight. No one other than Jerry and Doreen Rawlins encouraged me to fight for my life the way Robin did.

I wasn't mature enough to fix the broken things in our relationship and when things spiraled out of control, we were both at a loss trying to figure out how to fix our marriage. We both listened to advice about marriage and relationships from people who had no evidence in their own lives of a successful marriage. We divorced in 2008, four years after the shooting in October of 2004.

Robin was the primary contributor to making sure our children were balanced and focused, and I give the credit to her. I was busy trying to make life happen. Our kids are good kids, and they had good friends. I'm proud of them. They both have respect for law enforcement, and both had an interest in law enforcement and corrections careers.

Robin Wilson will always be a HERO in my journey through change.

Conrad's children, Bryson & McKenzie

Bryson

My son Bryson is an awesome young man and I'm so proud of him. He is a stout young man. I guess he took his size from the other side of the family. Bryson belonged to Boys Club, and he was a standout in Boys Club sports. He is an all-around athlete; he played baseball, basketball, and football. Bryson was an outgoing kid, a magnet.

In junior high, Bryson became a standout running back and baseball player. He focused on football in the fall, and in the spring, he focused on baseball. He was also a great basketball player.

I didn't force basketball on him, but I'd been coaching Bryson and his best friend, Jason until they reached junior high. When Bryson went to high school, he became an amazing baseball player; I mean he could knock the cover off the ball every game. From his sophomore year to his senior year, he would hit home runs in every game. He was that good. In football, he led the state in rushing yards as a junior and led the state his senior year as a running back in rushing. They selected Bryson just as they selected me to the state all-star team where they pick the cream of the crop. He played in the Les Schwab All-Star game at Civic Stadium in Portland.

Major colleges recruited Bryson, but because his grades weren't top-notch, he decided to take the junior college route. He attended College of the Siskiyous, a junior college in Northern California. The college fed players into San Francisco and San Jose State. He was on track to go to a major university, but during his time there he tired of football. He transferred to Southern Oregon University where he played one year, then grew away from football. He received his degree in Criminology.

Bryson is extremely successful, and he has an entrepreneurial spirit. He and Jason Summers, his best friend and business partner own a professional landscaping and irrigation company. He is a good kid; he stayed out of trouble and was never a problem. I'm a proud papa. He's done a wonderful job with his life. Bryson has his mother's personality and his drive came from me. He's my mini-me, I love him with everything I have, and I see myself in him.

Jason Summers, Bryson and Conrad

Conrad and Bryson Wilson

McKenzi

My beautiful daughter, McKenzi.

McKenzi was Little Miss Oregon when she was a young girl. My wife put her in ballet and tap and dance. McKenzi was a social butterfly. She was super cute; you know everybody says this about their child, but she was. The Little Miss Oregon pageant recruited her, and she traveled to Dallas, Texas and to other cities and competed in pageants and it helped shape her life. Sports helped keep her grounded.

McKenzi is also athletic; she played basketball in junior high and volleyball through high school.

I coached club volleyball for McKenzi's team from the time she was in third grade through the end of seventh grade. McKenzi was a good basketball player and she had such a kindred spirit. She wasn't aggressive until she got into middle school. She became a standout point guard, and she understood the game because in our house we talk sports.

In the driveway, we played one-on-one many times. McKenzi is tenacious, but she was also a girly-girl. She didn't want to break her nails. She played high school basketball for McKay high school and she was a skilled player. The team wasn't great, but they had a good coach. McKenzi also played volleyball from middle school through high school. She was athletic and talented, and she kept involved in school and sports.

McKenzi is doing well; she completed her education and works as a manager with the Department of Justice. McKenzi is married to my wonderful son-in-law, Josh Riddell. I've known him since he was around 10 years old. Josh is a remarkable young man, he played quarterback at Mississippi State and coaches high school football.

Josh and McKenzi look like Prince Harry and his wife, Meghan Markle. Josh has red hair and freckles and they have an amazing love story. I have royalty in my family because of the mix of my two children. I have a two-year-old granddaughter named Harper, and McKenzi recently gave birth to my second granddaughter, Halle. McKenzi is doing great and I love her dearly. I'm so proud of her and I love her family.

Harper, Halle and McKenzi Riddell

Halle & Harper Riddell

A Mentor is
someone who
allows you to
see the hope
within yourself.

- Oprah Winfrey

Mentors

Bob McMillan was my seventh-grade basketball coach. Bob spent a lot of time with me and recognized I was a good athlete when I came into middle school. He knew I had a difficult childhood, and my home life was not good. Bob took me under his wing. On lunch hours we would go into the gym, just the two of us and play one-on-one basketball. When I got in trouble in class, or whenever something didn't go right during the three years I was in middle school, I would be sent to the office to talk with Bob McMillan.

I played varsity basketball throughout middle school and Bob was the junior high varsity coach. He recognized my talent, and he could see my emotions were out of control. I had a chip on my shoulder. He saw in me a lost young man, and he wanted to pour into my life. And he did. He was there for me; he gave me some great tips and we're still friends to this day. Each year in Salem, Oregon they have a big 3-on-3 basketball event called The Hoopla, the 2nd largest event of its kind in the United States. Bob and I are still connected, and I volunteer as a referee each August for the three-day tournament. He was a difference maker, and I'm grateful for him.

Bob introduced me to my high school coach, Vic Backlund at McNary High School. Vic also knew my story, and after every game Coach Backland would talk with me. He knew things were difficult at home, and he gave me a ride home after every game if I didn't have a ride. Vic acted as a father figure for me. He taught me things a father should teach his child.

When I was a sophomore, Vic Backlund cosigned for my first set of wheels and tires for my car. I paid for them, but he cosigned for me to get credit. To this day, Vic Backlund and I are friends. He's a snowbird, he lives in Oregon but comes to Arizona in the summer and winter months. We make a point to see each other whenever we can.

My godparents, Jerry, and Doreen Rawlins. Jerry was the chaplain for the Portland Trail Blazers when Rick Adelman was the head coach. They have been in my life since the age of thirteen, and they're in my life now. We talk regularly; they send birthday cards, and they've done wonderful things for me throughout my life.

When Rick Adelman took a sabbatical from the Portland Trail Blazers, Jerry was his assistant coach at the junior college when we won the national championship. Jerry and I became acquainted, and our bond of friendship has never been broken. My wife and I got married in Mexico, and Jerry and Doreen wanted us to have a wedding in the US. They paid for the whole wedding, inviting family from around the United States. They taught me the principles of being a Christian and the principles of being a man. They owned a Savings and Loan company where my wife of twenty-two years started as a receptionist, and promoted to branch manager.

They impacted our lives in so many ways. I am indebted to them forever, and they won't let me pay them back anything monetarily. They said to me, "we call it Twig Bending", so I asked what is Twig Bending? And Doreen said, "just like when twigs are bent into different shapes, we're shaping you, and providing a future for you and your family. We're going to teach you to fish, we're not giving you a fish".

I learned later on in life; they were preparing me for what was coming next. They said in order for you to pay us back; you will give what we've given you. And it's my life mission, I give what was given to me. It comes naturally because they poured it into me. I'm still a great athlete, but I don't have the knees to move like I used to. Now I give through counseling, mentoring, player development, and through the coaching young athletes.

I give through speaking; I give through expression; I give through being a mentor; I give through being a coach. I feel every time I give; I give my best because they gave me their best. Jerry and Doreen Rawlins are the reason I am the man I am. They shaped me through sports. They were with me through the darkest part of my life. When I had tragic times, they called me every single day, three and four times a day. To encourage me, to provide hope and direction. And it paid off. I could see, I was blind but now I see.

I think about those people who poured into me, teachers and coaches and people outside my immediate family. Our children spend a lot of time in school and in sports. It's amazing when you have people pour into you when you have a difficult home life. Something many people may not realize is how important my mentors were. They weren't just coaches and teachers. They helped me to believe in myself and gave me what I needed and wasn't getting at home.

They were angels in disguise, all of these people. It doesn't happen, not where you get one after another. There is a beautiful picture of people who were there for me. It's incredible.

When I left Oregon and headed to Los Angeles, Jerry Rawlins and I stayed connected. He sent me stipends, so I could survive in Los Angeles. Every month like clockwork, he sent me financial aid to help me realize my dream. They had three sons of their own, who were like brothers to me. What an experience! I'm so grateful for them, and all the other people I may have failed to mention to you. There were so many people beyond my comprehension, instrumental to where I am sitting here today.

By telling my story, it is easy to see how they had a profound impact. They helped me to become successful, no matter what my circumstances were. People poured into me who had no other reason other than wanting to love on this troubled young kid. I was fortunate people kept picking me up. It makes me emotional, it's good to revisit and just be thankful.

Jerry & Doreen Rawlins

Jerry Rawlins and Conrad Wilson

There will come
a time when you
believe
everything is
finished.

That will be the
beginning.

- Annonymous

CHAPTER TEN

Full Circle

Just when you think you have it figured out, you find out things are not going to happen the way you had always envisioned.

In late 2018, I was traveling from Phoenix and happened to be in the Salem are where my father and my sister live. I was driving through the old neighborhood on my way to a rental property I own. I noticed my sister's car in his driveway, and I felt something telling me to stop and get out.

I parked the car and walked to the door. As I rang the doorbell, the little dogs he used to have were no longer there barking, and it was kind of an eerie, weird feeling. His wife Jenny answered the door, and I said "hey, is Dad around?" She was surprised to see me and I embraced her. My sister LaSonya also came to the door. I hugged my sister and she led me down the hallway to where my father was laying in the bedroom. As I entered the bedroom, he turned down the volume on his TV and we started talking. The next thing I know, he is apologizing – saying I'm sorry for never recognizing you for all of these years. You are the apple of my eye but I didn't know how to let you know I admired you, but I always did. He started crying and apologizing for all of the wrong he had done and the pain he inflicted stealing me from my mother. He went deep into how he had changed the course of my life and how proud he was of how I had overcome the many challenges and obstacles in my life. He told me he felt he had set me up for failure by taking me from my mother at such a young age.

I just sat there and listened, and when he was done apologizing, we had a word of prayer. When it was over, I said "I'm good", and he said he was ok. He was crying and my sister was crying. I told them when I leave here today, the past is behind us.

There is a sports analogy which says you need to have short term memory if you are going to succeed in life. Someone is going to hurt you. You might stumble, you might have a difficult journey, it could be many different things. But you need to learn to move past those hurtful things in order to grow and prosper.

I looked him in the eye and told him he taught me to succeed against the odds. If he had not taught me the only way he knew how to be, I would have never known how to counteract it and make myself become something better. For me, the negative stimulation increased my drive and ability to succeed. I've had more ups than downs. As

I left the room, he said he was super proud of me and I was the greatest accomplishment in his life.

I think it released me. He said he thought he was nearing his last days, and this was his opportunity to get it right before he crossed over to the afterlife.

I'm fortunate to have had the experience. At the time, it gave me the closure I needed. When I left his house, I started to receive text messages thanking me for praying with my dad. The visit influenced more than just me and my father, the text messages were a testimony of other people who were impacted by the meeting.

I've always been afraid to go to his house, he had always told us if we crossed him, he would kill us. But on this day, I was not scared, I was at the right place at the right time.

I was deeply moved by his apology, I felt like I was on the outside looking in, observing. It was like I scored the winning shot in a game at the very last second. I finally stepped over, I have no malice in my heart toward him.

My father was supposed to teach me how to be a man, but it's not how my story was written. I believe I am here to provide encouragement to others by sharing my story.

After this meeting, I had renewed hope. I thought it was a start to rebuilding a relationship with him. When I met with him and he apologized for all the pain and suffering and the disrespect he had shown me and demonstrated over the course of my life, and he said he had some remnants of jealousy because I succeeded without his help. I thought it was a new beginning.

For the first time in my life, I was optimistic I could forge a relationship with my father. I traveled back to Salem shortly after our emotional meeting. I had even decided to stay at his house for the first time in my adult life.

I slept with my suitcase propped against the door and I couldn't sleep but two or three hours at a time because I was having these weird vibrations about what I know him to be.

It was fine at the beginning. I stayed there a couple of days before he started nitpicking me and bringing up things which had happened 30, 40, 50 years ago.

He kept giving me little digs and I kept putting him off. The next evening my father had some guests over to his house. There were some people from the local church, a friend and his wife, my father, his wife Jenny, and myself.

My father has always been a gun guy. He carries this little Derringer pistol. It must have fallen out of his pocket somewhere in the house and once he noticed it was missing, he immediately started searching for it. No one knew what he was looking for at first until Jenny mentioned he lost the Derringer. We helped in the search and even turned the couch upside down looking for it, and no one could find it.

When we didn't find the gun, everyone went back to visiting, until he started yelling "You M***** F*****! You stole my gun! You're so privileged, you can ride on any airplane and get the gun through customs" and he went on, just yelling and talking crazy.

Everyone looked at me, and they were saying what's going on with this man? He was cussing at me and he was angry. I immediately told them I'm leaving. The people from the church wanted to pray. I felt like I was in danger, and I knew I had to leave.

I thought it was safe to stay at his home, it was disheartening after he apologized for the past.

He's still my parent. Even as an adult, I found myself looking for validation from him. I needed his apology at the time, and now I'm ready to move forward and get to the next level.

I can stand tall and say I've done everything I could for this relationship. I got what I needed, his apology and acknowledgment and now I can move on with my life.

I am changing, I have been constantly changing my whole life. I have been blessed with mentors and friends who have helped me to see there was more out there for me. I am ready to love myself and give grace and forgiveness which has been shown to me in so many ways.

I'm setting boundaries and respecting myself enough to say I have forgiven, and I don't have to live in the stories of my past

No matter where you are in life, you can move forward from the people and things which try to hold you back. I equate his behavior to a crab in a bucket; he doesn't want anybody to climb out and see the Mountaintop. He wants everyone to stay in the bucket with him.

It's okay to quit doing something if it's not prosperous for you. We have these transitions in our lives to make us better. I think it's important to help people get to where they need to go. We all have stories, and it's our responsibility to share our experiences and help others in their time of sorrow and strife.

I wouldn't change anything in my life, everything happened just the way it was supposed to happen - including him. I can rest in peace knowing I've done my best.

I feel like my life has gone full circle from the time I was a child until today. I don't have to question what kind of a person my father is anymore, I know for myself. I have validation. Now I can move forward and I don't have to ever think back and say he never took accountability or he never told me the truth. I finally got it from him. I don't need to look in the rearview mirror anymore.

I wish him well, God bless him. I will honor him as my father, but I will never be known as Larry Wilson again. My name is Conrad Wilson.

People saw something in me I didn't see in myself. I'm grateful for the people in my life who were the difference makers. Now I'm mature enough to understand it, and it's my mission to help others who are hurting. I want to be a life changer for someone else, just the way so many people were life changers for me.

I have work to do. I appreciate the process I've gone through. It hasn't been easy; it's been emotional and heart-wrenching.

I was forged in the fire of circumstance and I survived.

Help and Guidance

Talking with someone about your thoughts and feelings can save your life.

If you have been a victim of abuse or have suicidal thoughts please reach out for help. There is hope and help to heal from trauma. Please know you are never alone.

If you're thinking about suicide, are worried about a friend or loved one, or would like emotional support, the Lifeline network is available 24/7 across the United States. **800.273.8255**

Rape, Abuse, and Incest National Network (RAINN) National Sexual Assault Hotline - **800.656.HOPE**

Resources and help for men who have had unwanted or abusive sexual experiences in childhood.
https://1in6.org/helpline/

National support designed specifically for African-American men and women who were abused as children.
Black Sexual Abuse Survivors

Make A Safety Plan

A safety plan is designed to guide you through a crisis. As you continue through the steps, you can get help and feel safer. Keep your plan easily accessible in case you have thoughts of hurting yourself.

Recognize your personal warning signs: What thoughts, images, moods, situations, and behaviors indicate to you that a crisis may be developing? Write these down in your own words.

Use your own coping strategies: List things that you can do on your own to help you not act on urges to harm yourself.

Socialize with others who may offer support as well as distraction from the crisis: List people and social settings that may help take your mind off of difficult thoughts or feelings.

Contact family members or friends who may help to resolve a crisis: Make a list of people who are supportive and who you feel you can talk to when under stress.

Contact mental health professionals or agencies: Make a list of names, numbers and/or locations of clinicians, local emergency rooms, and crisis hotlines. Put the Lifeline number, 1-800-273-8255, into your phone.

Ensure your environment is safe: Have you thought of ways in which you might harm yourself? Work with a counselor to develop a plan to limit your access to these means.

For additional resources, visit
http://suicidepreventionlifeline.org/help-yourself/

COACH CONRAD WILSON

Coach Conrad Wilson is a motivational speaker, author, mentor and coach. Connect with Coach Conrad at www.conradwilson.com

Thank You

I would be remiss if I didn't thank Coach Conrad for sharing his story with me so we could share it with you.

Conrad Wilson is living proof of someone who forged success regardless of the past, and continues to give of himself so others may find hope and healing. You do not have to be a victim of your circumstance; it is a truth he lives each day.

My dream is for you to rise above situations which have held you back from your true potential. If you are hurting please use the resources listed in this book to reach out for help. Please know YOU matter.

Conrad, thank you for being vulnerable, for the laughter and even for the tears. The time we have worked together on this book has been a true blessing and it opened my eyes and my heart.

I am honored to call Conrad my friend, and I know we will be friends for a lifetime.

Julie Pershing

JULIE PERSHING

Julie Pershing is a writer, author, and the founder of Gallivant Press. Connect with Julie at hello@gallivantpress.com.

We bring your story to life

www.gallivantpress.com

Made in the USA
Columbia, SC
10 January 2022

53186765R00078